50 Bite Me, I'm Delicious Recipes

By: Kelly Johnson

Table of Contents

- Sassy Sriracha Shrimp Tacos
- Garlic Butter Vampire-Repelling Knots
- Mac Attack Truffle Mac & Cheese
- Hot Mess Jalapeño Poppers
- Slap Yo' Mama Fried Chicken
- Seductive Strawberry Shortcake
- Spicy AF Dragon Noodles
- Nacho Average Nachos
- Honey, I Burnt the Brussels (On Purpose)
- Sinfully Cheesy Pull-Apart Bread
- Bang Bang Cauliflower Bites
- Freakin' Good Fried Pickles
- Smokin' Bourbon BBQ Ribs
- Ooey Gooey Lava Cake
- Gimme S'more Cookie Skillet
- Can't-Stop-Won't-Stop Buffalo Dip
- Sweet 'n' Sticky Korean Wings

- Waffle Me Up Chicken Sandwich
- Bacon-Wrapped Everything
- Thicc 'n' Juicy Smash Burgers
- Pancakes of the Gods
- Unicorn Poop Sugar Cookies
- Crunchtastic Chili Cheese Fries
- Totally Loaded Breakfast Burrito
- Poppin' Pepperoni Pizza Bombs
- One Night Stand Spaghetti
- Cheater's 5-Minute Mug Cake
- I'm Nacho Girlfriend Queso
- Gooey Cinnamon Roll Bliss
- Brunch Beast Breakfast Tacos
- Fistful of Fudge Brownies
- Salty Bae Salted Caramel Pretzel Bites
- Kiss My Grits Cheesy Casserole
- Buttery AF Lobster Rolls
- OMG Oreo Cheesecake Bars
- Dangerously Devourable Dumplings

- Mac Me Up Mac & Cheese Balls
- Sticky Fingers Honey Garlic Wings
- Tomato Basil Bad Boy Soup
- Can't Even Caramel Apple Crisp
- Comfort Me Creamy Risotto
- Sweet Talkin' Teriyaki Beef Skewers
- What the Cluck Chicken Parm Sliders
- Spankin' Spaghetti Carbonara
- Don't Tell Grandma Apple Pie
- Broke Ramen Upgrade
- Muffin Compares to You Blueberry Muffins
- Dirty Dirty Dirty Chai Cupcakes
- Extra Thicc Chocolate Chip Cookies
- Lick the Spoon Lemon Bars

Sassy Sriracha Shrimp Tacos

Ingredients:

- Shrimp (peeled and deveined)
- Olive oil
- Sriracha
- Lime juice
- Garlic powder
- Salt
- Corn tortillas
- Shredded cabbage
- Cilantro
- Sour cream or crema

Instructions:

1. Toss shrimp with olive oil, sriracha, lime juice, garlic powder, and salt.
2. Sauté over medium heat until pink and cooked through.
3. Warm tortillas and fill with shrimp, cabbage, and cilantro.
4. Drizzle with sour cream or crema before serving.

Garlic Butter Vampire-Repelling Knots

Ingredients:

- Refrigerated biscuit dough or pizza dough
- Butter
- Fresh garlic, minced
- Parsley, chopped
- Parmesan cheese
- Salt

Instructions:

1. Roll dough into strips, tie into knots.
2. Bake at 375°F until golden brown.
3. While baking, melt butter and mix with garlic and parsley.
4. Brush hot knots with garlic butter and sprinkle with Parmesan and salt.

Mac Attack Truffle Mac & Cheese

Ingredients:

- Elbow macaroni
- Butter
- Flour
- Milk
- Heavy cream
- Cheddar, Gruyère, and Parmesan cheeses
- Truffle oil
- Salt and pepper

Instructions:

1. Cook macaroni and set aside.
2. In a saucepan, make a roux with butter and flour.
3. Slowly whisk in milk and cream until smooth and thickened.
4. Stir in cheeses until melted.
5. Add truffle oil, salt, and pepper.
6. Mix in pasta and serve hot.

Hot Mess Jalapeño Poppers

Ingredients:

- Jalapeños, halved and seeded
- Cream cheese
- Cheddar cheese
- Garlic powder
- Bacon strips
- Optional: hot sauce

Instructions:

1. Mix cream cheese, cheddar, and garlic powder.
2. Stuff jalapeño halves with cheese mixture.
3. Wrap each with bacon.
4. Bake at 400°F until bacon is crispy.
5. Drizzle with hot sauce if desired.

Slap Yo' Mama Fried Chicken

Ingredients:

- Chicken pieces (bone-in, skin-on)
- Buttermilk
- Hot sauce
- Flour
- Paprika, garlic powder, onion powder, cayenne, salt, pepper
- Oil for frying

Instructions:

1. Soak chicken in buttermilk and hot sauce overnight.
2. Mix flour with seasonings.
3. Dredge chicken in seasoned flour.
4. Fry in hot oil (350°F) until golden brown and cooked through.

Seductive Strawberry Shortcake
Ingredients:

- Fresh strawberries, sliced
- Sugar
- Heavy whipping cream
- Vanilla extract
- Shortcake biscuits or sponge cake

Instructions:

1. Mix strawberries with sugar and let sit.
2. Whip cream with vanilla and a little sugar until soft peaks form.
3. Slice shortcake, layer with strawberries and cream.
4. Serve immediately.

Spicy AF Dragon Noodles

Ingredients:

- Ramen or lo mein noodles
- Garlic, minced
- Soy sauce
- Brown sugar
- Sriracha
- Sesame oil
- Crushed red pepper
- Green onions
- Scrambled egg (optional)

Instructions:

1. Cook noodles and drain.
2. In a pan, sauté garlic in sesame oil.
3. Add soy sauce, brown sugar, sriracha, and red pepper.
4. Toss in noodles and stir to coat.
5. Mix in green onions and scrambled egg if using.

Nacho Average Nachos

Ingredients:

- Tortilla chips
- Shredded cheese (cheddar, Monterey Jack)
- Cooked ground beef or beans
- Jalapeños, sliced
- Sour cream
- Guacamole
- Salsa
- Green onions

Instructions:

1. Layer chips with cheese and beef/beans on a baking tray.
2. Bake at 375°F until cheese is melted.
3. Top with jalapeños, sour cream, guacamole, salsa, and green onions.
4. Serve hot and melty.

Honey, I Burnt the Brussels (On Purpose)
Ingredients:

- Brussels sprouts, halved
- Olive oil
- Honey
- Balsamic vinegar
- Salt and pepper
- Red pepper flakes (optional)

Instructions:

1. Toss Brussels sprouts with olive oil, salt, and pepper.
2. Roast at high heat (425°F) until crispy and charred in spots.
3. Drizzle with honey and balsamic vinegar, toss gently.
4. Sprinkle red pepper flakes if you like a kick. Serve warm.

Sinfully Cheesy Pull-Apart Bread
  Ingredients:

- Loaf of bread (like sourdough or Italian)
- Butter, melted
- Garlic, minced
- Mozzarella, cheddar, or any melty cheese
- Fresh herbs (parsley, chives)

Instructions:

1. Cut bread into a grid pattern without slicing all the way through.
2. Mix butter and garlic, brush into the cuts.
3. Stuff cheese into the crevices.
4. Wrap in foil and bake at 350°F until cheese melts.
5. Sprinkle fresh herbs and serve warm.

Bang Bang Cauliflower Bites

Ingredients:

- Cauliflower florets
- Flour
- Cornstarch
- Water
- Mayonnaise
- Sweet chili sauce
- Sriracha
- Garlic powder

Instructions:

1. Make batter with flour, cornstarch, water, and garlic powder.
2. Dip cauliflower in batter, then fry until golden and crispy.
3. Mix mayo, sweet chili sauce, and sriracha for the bang bang sauce.
4. Toss fried cauliflower in sauce and serve immediately.

Freakin' Good Fried Pickles

Ingredients:

- Dill pickle slices
- Flour
- Cornmeal
- Egg
- Buttermilk
- Cajun seasoning
- Oil for frying

Instructions:

1. Soak pickles in buttermilk.
2. Mix flour, cornmeal, and Cajun seasoning.
3. Dip pickles in egg, then dredge in flour mixture.
4. Fry in hot oil until crispy and golden.
5. Serve with ranch or spicy dipping sauce.

Smokin' Bourbon BBQ Ribs

Ingredients:

- Pork ribs
- Your favorite BBQ rub
- Bourbon
- BBQ sauce
- Smoked paprika

Instructions:

1. Rub ribs with BBQ rub and smoked paprika.
2. Slow cook or bake covered at low temp (275°F) for a few hours until tender.
3. Brush with bourbon and BBQ sauce, then grill or broil briefly to caramelize.
4. Serve with extra sauce on the side.

Ooey Gooey Lava Cake
Ingredients:

- Semi-sweet chocolate
- Butter
- Sugar
- Eggs
- Flour
- Vanilla extract
- Powdered sugar (optional)

Instructions:

1. Melt chocolate and butter together.
2. Whisk eggs and sugar until fluffy.
3. Fold chocolate mixture into eggs, then add flour and vanilla.
4. Pour into ramekins and bake at 425°F for about 12 minutes (edges set, center soft).
5. Dust with powdered sugar and serve warm.

Gimme S'more Cookie Skillet

Ingredients:

- Chocolate chip cookie dough
- Mini marshmallows
- Graham crackers, crushed
- Chocolate chunks

Instructions:

1. Press cookie dough into a cast-iron skillet.
2. Sprinkle marshmallows, chocolate chunks, and graham cracker crumbs on top.
3. Bake at 350°F until golden and marshmallows toasted.
4. Serve warm, scoop it out!

Can't-Stop-Won't-Stop Buffalo Dip
Ingredients:

- Cooked shredded chicken
- Cream cheese
- Buffalo sauce
- Ranch or blue cheese dressing
- Shredded cheddar cheese
- Green onions

Instructions:

1. Mix shredded chicken with cream cheese, buffalo sauce, and ranch/blue cheese dressing.
2. Spread in a baking dish, top with cheddar.
3. Bake at 350°F until bubbly and melted.
4. Garnish with green onions and serve with chips or celery sticks.

Sweet 'n' Sticky Korean Wings

Ingredients:

- Chicken wings
- Soy sauce
- Gochujang (Korean chili paste)
- Honey
- Garlic, minced
- Ginger, minced
- Sesame oil
- Sesame seeds
- Green onions

Instructions:

1. Toss wings in soy sauce, gochujang, honey, garlic, ginger, and sesame oil.
2. Bake or fry wings until cooked and crispy.
3. Toss again in sauce if needed for extra stickiness.
4. Garnish with sesame seeds and chopped green onions.

Waffle Me Up Chicken Sandwich

Ingredients:

- Fried chicken breast
- Waffles (use as buns)
- Maple syrup
- Butter
- Lettuce, tomato, pickles (optional)

Instructions:

1. Prepare waffles and fry chicken.
2. Butter waffles lightly and drizzle with maple syrup.
3. Assemble sandwich with chicken and optional veggies.
4. Serve warm and enjoy the sweet-savory combo.

Bacon-Wrapped Everything
Ingredients:

- Bacon strips

- Ingredients to wrap (jalapeños, shrimp, asparagus, dates, or mini sausages)

Instructions:

1. Wrap bacon tightly around chosen ingredients.

2. Secure with toothpicks if needed.

3. Bake at 400°F until bacon is crisp.

4. Serve as a delicious finger food or appetizer.

Thicc 'n' Juicy Smash Burgers

Ingredients:

- Ground beef (80/20)
- Salt and pepper
- Cheese slices
- Burger buns
- Toppings: lettuce, tomato, pickles, onions, sauce

Instructions:

1. Form loosely packed balls of beef.
2. Smash on hot griddle or skillet to form thin patties.
3. Cook until crispy edges form, flip and add cheese.
4. Assemble with buns and toppings.

Pancakes of the Gods

Ingredients:

- Flour
- Baking powder
- Sugar
- Milk
- Eggs
- Butter, melted
- Vanilla extract
- Toppings: berries, syrup, whipped cream

Instructions:

1. Mix dry ingredients, then add wet ingredients and stir gently.
2. Cook pancakes on hot griddle until bubbles form, flip and cook through.
3. Stack pancakes and top with berries, syrup, and whipped cream.

Unicorn Poop Sugar Cookies
Ingredients:

- Sugar cookie dough (homemade or store-bought)
- Food coloring (various bright colors)
- Sprinkles and edible glitter

Instructions:

1. Divide dough into portions and color each with food coloring.
2. Twist colored doughs together and shape into small logs or rounds.
3. Bake at 350°F until edges are just golden.
4. Decorate with sprinkles and edible glitter for that magical vibe.

Crunchtastic Chili Cheese Fries

Ingredients:

- Frozen or fresh fries
- Chili (your favorite recipe or canned)
- Shredded cheddar cheese
- Jalapeños (optional)
- Sour cream and green onions for topping

Instructions:

1. Cook fries until crispy.
2. Top fries with hot chili and shredded cheese.
3. Broil briefly to melt cheese.
4. Garnish with jalapeños, sour cream, and green onions.

Totally Loaded Breakfast Burrito
Ingredients:

- Large flour tortilla
- Scrambled eggs
- Crispy bacon or sausage
- Shredded cheese
- Hash browns
- Salsa or hot sauce
- Avocado (optional)

Instructions:

1. Layer all ingredients in tortilla.
2. Fold sides and roll tightly.
3. Optional: grill burrito on skillet to seal and warm through.
4. Serve with extra salsa or sour cream.

Poppin' Pepperoni Pizza Bombs

Ingredients:

- Refrigerated biscuit dough or pizza dough
- Pepperoni slices
- Mozzarella cheese, shredded
- Pizza sauce
- Italian seasoning

Instructions:

1. Flatten dough pieces, layer with pepperoni and cheese, and a spoonful of pizza sauce.
2. Fold dough around fillings and pinch to seal.
3. Bake at 375°F until golden and puffed.
4. Serve warm with extra pizza sauce for dipping.

One Night Stand Spaghetti

Ingredients:

- Spaghetti noodles
- Olive oil
- Garlic, minced
- Crushed red pepper flakes
- Cherry tomatoes, halved
- Parmesan cheese
- Fresh basil

Instructions:

1. Cook spaghetti until al dente.
2. Sauté garlic and red pepper flakes in olive oil.
3. Add cherry tomatoes and cook until soft.
4. Toss pasta with sauce, sprinkle with Parmesan and basil.
5. Serve immediately.

Cheater's 5-Minute Mug Cake

Ingredients:

- Flour
- Sugar
- Cocoa powder
- Baking powder
- Milk
- Vegetable oil
- Vanilla extract

Instructions:

1. Mix dry ingredients in a mug.
2. Stir in milk, oil, and vanilla.
3. Microwave for about 1-2 minutes until set.
4. Let cool slightly and enjoy.

I'm Nacho Girlfriend Queso

Ingredients:

- Velveeta or processed cheese
- Diced tomatoes and green chilies
- Jalapeños
- Ground chorizo or sausage (optional)
- Green onions

Instructions:

1. Melt cheese in a pot over low heat.
2. Stir in diced tomatoes, chilies, jalapeños, and cooked chorizo.
3. Garnish with green onions and serve warm with tortilla chips.

Gooey Cinnamon Roll Bliss

Ingredients:

- Refrigerated cinnamon roll dough
- Butter
- Brown sugar
- Cinnamon
- Cream cheese icing (included or homemade)

Instructions:

1. Arrange cinnamon rolls in a baking dish.
2. Bake according to package instructions.
3. Drizzle with extra butter and brown sugar glaze if desired.
4. Top with cream cheese icing and serve warm.

Brunch Beast Breakfast Tacos

Ingredients:

- Scrambled eggs
- Crispy bacon or sausage
- Shredded cheese
- Salsa
- Flour or corn tortillas
- Avocado slices

Instructions:

1. Warm tortillas.
2. Fill with eggs, meat, cheese, and salsa.
3. Add avocado slices on top.
4. Fold and serve immediately.

Fistful of Fudge Brownies

Ingredients:

- Brownie mix or homemade batter
- Chocolate chips or chunks
- Nuts (optional)

Instructions:

1. Prepare brownie batter, fold in chips and nuts.
2. Bake according to recipe or package instructions.
3. Cut into generous squares and serve.

Salty Bae Salted Caramel Pretzel Bites

Ingredients:

- Mini pretzels
- Caramel candies
- Sea salt

Instructions:

1. Place pretzels on a baking sheet.
2. Top each with a caramel candy.
3. Bake at 350°F until caramel melts.
4. Sprinkle with sea salt and let cool slightly before serving.

Kiss My Grits Cheesy Casserole

Ingredients:

- Instant grits
- Cheddar cheese
- Cream cheese
- Milk
- Butter
- Bacon bits (optional)

Instructions:

1. Cook grits according to package.
2. Stir in cheeses, butter, and milk until creamy.
3. Pour into casserole dish, top with bacon bits if using.
4. Bake at 350°F until bubbly and golden.

Buttery AF Lobster Rolls

Ingredients:

- Cooked lobster meat, chopped
- Butter
- Soft hot dog buns or split-top rolls
- Mayonnaise
- Lemon juice
- Celery, finely chopped (optional)
- Salt and pepper
- Fresh parsley

Instructions:

1. Mix lobster meat with mayo, lemon juice, celery, salt, and pepper.
2. Butter the buns and toast them lightly in a pan.
3. Fill buns generously with lobster mixture.
4. Garnish with parsley and serve immediately.

OMG Oreo Cheesecake Bars

Ingredients:

- Oreo cookies (crushed for crust)
- Cream cheese
- Sugar
- Eggs
- Vanilla extract
- Additional crushed Oreos for topping

Instructions:

1. Press crushed Oreos into the bottom of a baking pan for the crust.
2. Beat cream cheese, sugar, eggs, and vanilla until smooth.
3. Pour over crust and bake at 325°F until set.
4. Sprinkle crushed Oreos on top before cooling completely.
5. Chill before slicing.

Dangerously Devourable Dumplings
Ingredients:

- Dumpling wrappers
- Ground pork or chicken
- Ginger, minced
- Garlic, minced
- Soy sauce
- Green onions, chopped
- Sesame oil

Instructions:

1. Mix filling ingredients together.
2. Place small spoonful on wrapper, fold and seal edges.
3. Pan-fry or steam dumplings until cooked through.
4. Serve with soy sauce or dipping sauce.

Mac Me Up Mac & Cheese Balls

Ingredients:

- Prepared mac & cheese (homemade or boxed)
- Flour
- Eggs
- Bread crumbs
- Oil for frying

Instructions:

1. Chill mac & cheese until firm.
2. Roll into balls, coat in flour, then egg, then bread crumbs.
3. Fry in hot oil until golden and crispy.
4. Drain and serve warm.

Sticky Fingers Honey Garlic Wings
Ingredients:

- Chicken wings
- Honey
- Garlic, minced
- Soy sauce
- Rice vinegar
- Sesame seeds

Instructions:

1. Bake or fry wings until cooked and crispy.
2. Mix honey, garlic, soy sauce, and vinegar in a pan; simmer until thickened.
3. Toss wings in sauce until coated.
4. Sprinkle with sesame seeds and serve.

Tomato Basil Bad Boy Soup

Ingredients:

- Tomatoes (fresh or canned)
- Onion, chopped
- Garlic, minced
- Fresh basil
- Vegetable broth
- Heavy cream (optional)
- Olive oil
- Salt and pepper

Instructions:

1. Sauté onion and garlic in olive oil.
2. Add tomatoes and broth, simmer.
3. Blend soup until smooth.
4. Stir in cream and fresh basil.
5. Season and serve hot.

Can't Even Caramel Apple Crisp

Ingredients:

- Apples, peeled and sliced
- Brown sugar
- Cinnamon
- Rolled oats
- Flour
- Butter
- Caramel sauce

Instructions:

1. Toss apples with brown sugar and cinnamon.
2. Place in baking dish.
3. Mix oats, flour, and butter until crumbly, sprinkle on apples.
4. Bake at 350°F until topping is golden.
5. Drizzle caramel sauce over warm crisp.

Comfort Me Creamy Risotto
Ingredients:

- Arborio rice
- Onion, finely chopped
- Garlic, minced
- Chicken or vegetable broth
- White wine (optional)
- Parmesan cheese
- Butter
- Olive oil
- Salt and pepper

Instructions:

1. Sauté onion and garlic in olive oil and butter.
2. Add rice and toast lightly.
3. Gradually add warm broth, stirring constantly until absorbed.
4. Stir in cheese and adjust seasoning.
5. Serve creamy and warm.

Sweet Talkin' Teriyaki Beef Skewers

Ingredients:

- Beef sirloin or flank steak, cut into cubes
- Teriyaki sauce
- Garlic, minced
- Ginger, minced
- Green onions (for garnish)
- Wooden skewers (soaked in water)

Instructions:

1. Marinate beef cubes in teriyaki sauce, garlic, and ginger for at least 1 hour.
2. Thread beef onto skewers.
3. Grill or broil until cooked to desired doneness.
4. Garnish with chopped green onions and serve.

What the Cluck Chicken Parm Sliders
Ingredients:

- Mini slider buns
- Breaded chicken cutlets, cooked and sliced
- Marinara sauce
- Mozzarella cheese
- Fresh basil leaves

Instructions:

1. Place a piece of chicken on each bun bottom.
2. Spoon marinara sauce over chicken.
3. Top with mozzarella cheese and basil.
4. Toast sliders in oven until cheese melts.
5. Assemble with bun tops and serve warm.

Spankin' Spaghetti Carbonara
 Ingredients:

- Spaghetti
- Eggs
- Parmesan cheese, grated
- Pancetta or bacon, diced
- Garlic, minced
- Black pepper

Instructions:

1. Cook spaghetti until al dente.
2. Fry pancetta/bacon until crispy; add garlic briefly.
3. Whisk eggs and Parmesan together.
4. Toss hot pasta with pancetta and garlic, then quickly stir in egg mixture off heat to create creamy sauce.
5. Season with black pepper and serve immediately.

Don't Tell Grandma Apple Pie

Ingredients:

- Pie crust (store-bought or homemade)
- Apples, peeled and sliced
- Sugar
- Cinnamon
- Nutmeg
- Butter
- Egg wash

Instructions:

1. Toss apples with sugar, cinnamon, and nutmeg.
2. Fill pie crust with apple mixture, dot with butter.
3. Cover with top crust, seal edges, and cut slits for steam.
4. Brush with egg wash.
5. Bake at 375°F until crust is golden and apples are tender.

Broke Ramen Upgrade
Ingredients:

- Instant ramen noodles
- Egg
- Green onions, chopped
- Soy sauce
- Sriracha or chili paste (optional)
- Frozen veggies or leftover cooked meat (optional)

Instructions:

1. Cook ramen noodles according to package, drain most of the water.
2. Stir in soy sauce, sriracha, and veggies or meat if using.
3. Crack an egg into the hot noodles and stir until cooked.
4. Garnish with green onions and serve hot.

Muffin Compares to You Blueberry Muffins
Ingredients:

- Flour
- Sugar
- Baking powder
- Salt
- Milk
- Eggs
- Butter, melted
- Fresh or frozen blueberries

Instructions:

1. Mix dry ingredients in one bowl, wet ingredients in another.
2. Combine gently and fold in blueberries.
3. Spoon batter into muffin tins.
4. Bake at 375°F until golden and a toothpick comes out clean.

Dirty Dirty Dirty Chai Cupcakes
Ingredients:

- Flour
- Sugar
- Baking soda
- Ground cinnamon, cardamom, ginger, cloves
- Black tea or chai concentrate
- Eggs
- Butter
- Vanilla extract

Instructions:

1. Mix dry ingredients including spices.
2. Combine wet ingredients, then add dry to wet.
3. Fill cupcake liners and bake at 350°F until a toothpick comes out clean.
4. Frost with chai-spiced buttercream or cream cheese frosting.

Extra Thicc Chocolate Chip Cookies
Ingredients:

- Flour
- Baking soda
- Salt
- Butter, softened
- Brown and white sugar
- Eggs
- Vanilla extract
- Chocolate chips

Instructions:

1. Cream butter and sugars.
2. Add eggs and vanilla.
3. Mix in dry ingredients.
4. Fold in chocolate chips.
5. Scoop large dollops onto baking sheet and bake at 350°F until golden but soft in the middle.

Lick the Spoon Lemon Bars
Ingredients:

- Flour
- Powdered sugar
- Butter
- Eggs
- Granulated sugar
- Fresh lemon juice and zest
- Baking powder

Instructions:

1. Make crust with flour, powdered sugar, and butter, press into pan and bake.
2. Whisk eggs, sugar, lemon juice, zest, and baking powder.
3. Pour over baked crust and bake until set.
4. Cool and dust with powdered sugar before slicing.

www.ingramcontent.com/pod-product-compliance
Lightning Source LLC
LaVergne TN
LVHW081323060526
838201LV00055B/2438